THE
WORLD'S
STUPIDEST
Last
Words

THE
WORLD'S
STUPIDEST
Last
Words

Michael O'Mara Humour

First published in Great Britain in 2004 by
Michael O'Mara Books Limited
9 Lion Yard, Tremadoc Road
London SW4 7NQ

A CIP catalogue record for this book is available
from the British Library

ISBN 1-84317-021-3

1 3 5 7 9 10 8 6 4 2

Designed and typeset by Design 23

Compiled by Rhian McKay and Chris Maynard

Printed and bound in Great Britain by Cox & Wyman Ltd,
Reading, Berkshire

www.mombooks.com

CONTENTS

**O, but they say the tongues
of dying men
Enforce attention, like
deep harmony**

– Shakespeare
Richard II,
II.i.5-6

INTRODUCTION

Death, the Grim Reaper, that old lightning bolt from the sky – whatever we call it, and whoever we are, it comes to us all eventually. Until science brings immortality to the human form (along with the abolition of taxes and the flying pig) then we will continue to shuffle off this mortal coil, and the utterances we make before drawing our final breath will continue to follow us to the grave, and possibly beyond.

Have you ever seriously thought about the words that you'd like those left behind to remember you by? Would you try for something profound, funny, cantankerous, or enigmatic? Philosophical, sarcastic, resigned or joyful? Hasn't crossed your mind? Evidently, it seems to have escaped some of the figures you'll find in this book too. But perhaps we shouldn't judge them too harshly – this is death we're talking about, after all, and it's not always easy!

So, when you feel that you're ready, take a deep breath, turn the page, and come face to face with some of the strangest, stupidest, most petulant or profound closing lines uttered by your fellow humans. Just try not to think about your own mortality in the process...

Going Out In Style

Vachel Lindsay, American poet,
suicide by drinking a bottle of
cleaning fluid 1931
'They tried to get me. I got them first!'

●

Ramon Maria Narvaez, Spanish Prime
Minister, died 1868 – when asked by a
priest whether he forgave his enemies
**'I do not have to forgive my enemies. I
have had them all shot.'**

●

There's only one way to find out...

Kenneth Rexroth, American twentieth-century poet – remembering his father's last words
'He said he was dying of fast women, slow horses, crooked cards and straight whisky.'

•

Spencer Perceval, British Prime Minister, assassinated 1812
'Murder!'

•

Yeah? Over my dead body...

Taki Zenzaburo, Japanese officer,
suicide by hara-kiri 1868
'I, and I alone, unwarrantably gave the
order to fire on the foreigners at Kobe,
and again as they tried to escape. For
this crime I disembowel myself, and I
beg you who are present to do me the
honour of witnessing the act.'

●

Richard III, King of England, killed 1485
'I will die King of England, I will not
budge a foot! Treason! Treason!'

●

*It's OK, they only attack when
they're hungry...*

Sir Richard Grenville, Elizabethan sailor, died of wounds 1591
'Here I die, Richard Grenville, with a joyful and quiet mind, for that I have ended my life as a good soldier ought to, who has fought for his country, Queen, religion and honour. Wherefore my soul most joyfully departeth out of this body...but the others of my company have done as traitors and dogs, for which they shall be reproached all their lives and leave a shameful name for ever.'

•

Julius Streicher, Nazi war criminal, hanged 1946
'Heil Hitler!'

•

I don't think anyone followed me...

Pierre Laval, France's collaborationist
Premier, executed by firing squad 1945
'Vive la France!'

•

James French, executed by electric
chair 1966
**'How about this for a headline for
tomorrow's paper: "French Fries"?'**

•

That doesn't look so hard...

G. W. Green, executed by lethal
injection 1991
'Lock and load. Let's do it.'

•

Isadora Duncan, dancer, killed 1927
'Adieu my friends, I go on to glory!'

•

OK, take your best shot...

William Hotman, soldier in the American Revolution, killed 1781 – as the British were attempting to blow up his fort and kill everyone inside, Hotman ruined the powder with the blood from his fatal wounds and saved his companions

'We will endeavour to crawl to this line, we will completely wet the powder with our blood; thus we will, with the life that remains in us, save the fort and the magazine and perhaps a few of our comrades who are only wounded.'

•

Archimedes, Greek mathematician, killed 212 BC – to the soldiers who broke into his room and killed him in cold blood
'Stand away, fellow, from my diagram!'

•

You clearly have no idea who you're dealing with...

Adolph Fischer, hanged after the 1886
Haymarket bombing, Chicago
**'Hurray for anarchy! This is the
happiest moment of my life.'**

•

Johnny Frank Garrett, executed by
lethal injection 1992
**'I'd like to thank my family for loving
me and taking care of me. And the rest
of the world can kiss my ass.'**

•

No, this cannot be. I'm invincible!

Georges Clemenceau, French Premier,
died 1929
**'I wish to be buried standing – facing
Germany.'**

•

Leon Czogolsz, assassin of President
McKinley, electrocuted 1901
**'I killed the President because he was
the enemy of the good people, the
good working people. I am not sorry
for my crime.'**

•

I'll get a world record for this...

The Duc de Lanzon de Biron, guillotined 1793 – asking the executioner for a few more minutes
'I beg a thousand pardons my friend, but permit me to finish this last dozen of oysters.'

•

John Philpot Curran, Irish writer and wit, died 1817 – replying to his doctor who commented, 'You are coughing with more difficulty'
'That is surprising, since I have been practising all night.'

•

Yes, I've decided, I'm going to cut the red wire first...

Edward I, King of England, died 1307
**'Carry my bones before you on
your march. For the rebels will not be
able to endure the sight of me,
alive or dead.'**

●

Gary Gilmore, executed by
firing squad 1977
'Let's do it!'

●

*It's easy, I'll just jump from
our car into his...*

Karl Marx, German philosopher and social theorist, died 1883 – upon being asked by his housekeeper whether he had any final words

'Get out! Last words are for fools who haven't said enough!'

•

Louis XIV, King of France, died 1781
'Why are you weeping? Did you imagine that I was immortal?'

•

It's not a problem, I've seen this done in the movies...

Jack Sheppard, thief, hanged 1724
'Of two virtues have I ever cherished an honest pride. Never have I stooped to friendship with Jonathan Wild or with any of his detestable thief-takers, and though an undutiful son, I never damned my mother's eyes.'

•

Dylan Thomas, poet, died 1953
'I've had eighteen straight whiskies, I think that's the record.
After thirty-nine years this is all I've done.'

•

No, don't worry, they cleared this minefield years ago...

Thomas J. Grasso, executed by lethal injection 1995
'I did not get my Spaghetti-Os, I got spaghetti. I want the press to know this.'

•

George V, King of England, died 1936 (attributed)
'Bugger Bognor!'

•

He's probably just hibernating...

Martin Luther, founder of
Protestantism, died 1546 – when asked
whether he still held his radical beliefs
'Yes!'

•

Charles Abbott, Lord Chief Justice,
died 1832 – addressing an
imaginary jury
**'Gentlemen, you are
all dismissed.'**

•

OK, let's see if this thing is loaded...

Lord Palmerston, British Prime Minister, died 1865 – upon being told by his doctor that he was going to die
'Die, my dear doctor?
That's the last thing I shall do!'

•

Jaroslav Hašek, Czech author, died 1923 – reproaching the doctor who refused him one final drink of brandy
'But you're cheating me!'

•

I thought you took care
of the guards?

Siward, Earl of Northumbria, died 1055
'Shame on me that I did not die in one of the many battles that I have fought, but am reserved to die with the disgrace of the death of a sick cow! At least put on my armour of proof, gird the sword by my side, place the helmet on my head, let me have my shield in my left hand and my gold-inlaid battleaxe in my right hand, that the bravest of soldiers may die in a soldier's garb.'

•

Anonymous, suicide by hanging
'That's all folks!'

•

It's no use, I think we'll have to reason with them...

Taking It In
Your Stride

Henry Fox, first Baron Holland, died 1774
**'If Mr Selwyn calls again, show him up.
If I am alive I shall be delighted to see
him, and if I am dead he would like to
see me.'**

•

Nancy Astor, British politician, died 1964
– upon waking on her deathbed to find
herself surrounded by her family
'Am I dying? Or is this my birthday?'

•

*Don't worry, I think it's just
a flesh wound...*

Jacques Vache, surrealist painter,
suicide 1919 – true to his word, he and
two friends killed themselves together
**'I shall die when I want to die. And
then shall die with someone else. To
die alone is boring. I should prefer to
die with one of my best friends.'**

●

James Quinn, British actor, died 1766
**'I could wish this tragic scene were
over, but I hope to go through it with
becoming modesty.'**

●

Don't be silly.
Of course I've disarmed it...

Ilya Mechnikov, Russian biologist,
died 1916
'You remember your promise?
You will do my post-mortem?
And look at the intestines carefully,
for I think there is something
there now.'

●

Socrates, suicide by drinking
hemlock 399 BC
'Crito, we owe a cock to Asclepius.
Pay it and do not neglect it.'

●

*Well, at least things can't
get any worse...*

William Hunter, professor of anatomy,
died 1783
**'If I had the strength to hold a pen,
I would write how easy and pleasant
it is to die.'**

•

George Appel, executed by electric
chair 1928
**'Well, gentlemen, you are about to
see a baked Appel.'**

•

*Strange. That's never
happened before...*

Johannes Brahms, German
composer, died 1897 – enjoying
a final glass of wine
'Ah, that tastes nice. Thank you.'

•

Edward, first Baron Thurlow,
Lord Chancellor of England,
died 1806
**'I'll be shot if I don't believe
I'm dying!'**

•

*According to the laws of probability,
this cannot fail...*

William Howard, first Viscount
Stafford, beheaded 1680
**'This block will be my pillow and I shall
repose there well without pain, grief,
or fear.'**

•

Nathan Hale, shot by the British as a
spy 1776
**'What a pity it is that we can die but
once to serve our country.'**

•

*We have a bit of a problem.
Can anybody else fly a plane?*

Francisco Franco Bahamonde,
Spanish general and statesman,
died 1975 – on his deathbed, upon
being told that General Garcia
wanted to say goodbye
'Why, is Garcia going on a trip?'

●

James Allen Red Dog, executed by
lethal injection 1993
'I'm going home, babe.'

●

*I'm sure it can't be
that dangerous...*

Oscar Wilde, dramatist and wit,
died 1900 (attributed)
'Either this wallpaper goes, or I do.'

●

David Hume, British philosopher,
economist and historian,
died 1776
**'I am dying as fast as my enemies,
if I have any, could wish, and as
cheerfully as my best friends
could desire.'**

●

*Let's see what happens when I
mix these two highly volatile
liquids together...*

Edmund Gwenn, Welsh actor, died 1959
– upon being asked by friend and
fellow actor Jack Lemmon whether it
was difficult to face death
**'It's hard, very hard indeed.
But not as hard as doing comedy!'**

•

Thomas Paine, political theorist, died
1809 – upon his doctor commenting,
'Your belly diminishes'
'And yours augments.'

•

Oops...

Frederick William I, King of Prussia, died 1740 – upon being read to from the Bible, 'Naked came I out of my mother's womb, and naked shall I return thither'

'No, not quite naked. I shall have my uniform on!'

•

Captain L. E. G. Oates, British explorer, died 1912
'I am just going outside, and may be some time.'

•

No problem, I have a cunning plan...

Zachary Taylor, US President,
died 1850
'I am about to die, I expect the summons soon. I have endeavoured to discharge all my official duties faithfully. I regret nothing, but am sorry that I am about to leave my friends.'

●

Benjamin Disraeli, British Prime Minister, died 1881
'I had rather live, but I'm not afraid to die.'

●

It probably just wants to be friends with us...

Dominique Bouhours, French
grammarian, died 1702
**'I am about to – or I am going to – die.
Either expression is used.'**

•

Gabriele D'Annunzio, Italian poet and
novelist, died 1938
'I'm bored, I'm bored!'

•

*Great! I've always wanted to
swim with sharks...*

Richard Monckton Milnes, British writer, politician and gourmet, died 1885
'My exit is the result of too many entrées.'

•

Thaddeus Stevens, American politician, died 1868 – upon being told by a visitor that he looked very pale
'It's not my appearance that troubles me now. It's my disappearance!'

•

Trust me, I'm an expert...

Marco Bozzari, Greek patriot,
died 1823
**'Oh, to die for liberty is a pleasure
and not a pain!'**

●

Alexander Pope, English poet and
satirist, died 1744 – upon being told
by his doctor that his vital signs
were very healthy
**'Here am I, dying of a hundred
good symptoms!'**

●

*Are you sure you checked that this
rope was tied properly?*

Dr Karl Brandt, Nazi war criminal, hanged 1948
'It is no shame to stand on this scaffold. I served my fatherland as others before me.'

•

James J. Walker, American politician, died 1946 – he refused his nurse's request for him to lie back until she admitted to sharing his Democratic Party beliefs
'In that case I shall abide by the wishes of a fair constituent.'

•

What instructions?

Allen Ginsberg, American poet,
died 1997 (attributed)
'Toodle-oo!'

•

Kathleen Ferrier, opera singer,
died 1953
'Now I'll have eine kleine pause.'

•

*I've beaten you once and
I'll do it again!*

Just A Minute!

Charlotte Brontë, writer, died during pregnancy 1855 – she had been married only one year
'Oh, I am not going to die, am I? He will not separate us, we have been so happy.'

•

Cecil Rhodes, South African statesman, died 1902
'So little done, so much to do.'

•

Well, at least we tried...

RMS *Titanic*, sunk 1912 – the final SOS
sent by the crew
**'Have struck iceberg.
Badly damaged. Rush aid.'**

•

Fitz-Greene Halleck, American poet,
died 1867
**'Maria, hand me my pantaloons,
if you please.'**

•

*Let me just have a look out of the
train window...*

Ethan Allen, American patriot, died
1789 – upon being told on his
deathbed that the angels were
waiting for him
**'Waiting, are they?
Well, let 'em wait.'**

•

James B. Eads, engineer, died 1887
**'I cannot die.
I have not finished my work.'**

•

*This bit goes in there?
Well, if you say so...*

Richard Savage, British poet, died 1743
– to his gaoler
**'I have something to say to you,
sir – 'tis gone!'**

•

Victor Emmanuel II, King of Italy,
died 1878
**'How much longer will it last? I have
some important things to attend to.'**

•

He's a big guy, isn't he?

Pancho Villa, Mexican revolutionary,
died 1923
'Don't let it end like this. Tell them I
said something!'

•

Johann George Jacobi, poet, died 1919
– after finishing on New Year's Eve a
poem about New Year's Day
'I shall not in fact see the New Year
which I have just commemorated.
I hope, at least, it is not apparent in
the poem how elderly I am.'

•

*Come on, you cowards.
There's nothing to be scared of...*

Manuel 'Three-fingered Jack' Garcia,
Mexican bandit, killed 1853
**'I will throw up my hands for no
gringo dog.'**

•

Henry Segrave, British sportsman,
killed 1930 – Segrave was attempting
to break the world speedboat record
when his boat crashed
'Did we do it?'

•

*They're not usually aggressive.
If we leave them alone,
they'll leave us alone...*

General John Sedgwick, shot during the Civil War 1864 – his last words, rallying his men
'Come on, men! They couldn't hit an elephant at this dist–'

•

Sir William Davenant, playwright and Poet Laureate, died 1668 – explaining why he could not conclude the poem he had been working on
'I shall have to ask leave to desist, when I am interrupted by so great an experiment as dying.'

•

Is that the best you can do?

Dr John Wolcot, 'Peter Pindar',
satirist, died 1819
'Give me back my youth.'

•

Emily Brontë, writer, died 1848
– after having refused her family's
urgings to call for a doctor
**'If you send for a doctor I will
see him now.'**

•

What happens if I press this?

Madame de Pompadour, French royal mistress and courtier, died 1764 – calling out to God to allow her time to apply rouge to her cheeks
'Wait a moment!'

●

James Joyce, Irish writer, died 1941
'Does nobody understand?'

●

Revenge will be mine...

George Bernard Shaw, dramatist and
Fabian, died 1950
– to his nurse
**'Sister, you're trying to keep me alive
as an old curiosity. But I'm done,
I'm finished. I'm going to die.'**

•

Katsushika Hokusai, Japanese painter,
died 1849
**'If Heaven had only granted me five
years more, I could have become a
real painter.'**

•

*Hold on! I'm coming
to save you...*

Philosophical Farewells

Pierre, Baron de Cambronne,
French general, led the Old Guard at
Waterloo, died 1842
**'Ah, mademoiselle, man is thought to
be something, but he is nothing.'**

●

Titus Oates, instigator of the
'Popish Plot' of 1678, died 1705
'It is all the same in the end.'

●

*He's about to jump from the top of
that thirteen-floor building.
I'll just run and catch him...*

Sir Isaac Newton, philosopher and mathematician, died 1727
'I don't know what I may seem to the world. But as to myself, I seem to have been only a boy playing on the seashore and diverting myself in now and then finding a smoother pebble or prettier shell than the ordinary, whilst the great ocean of truth lay all undiscovered before me.'

•

Hugo de Groot, Dutch jurist, statesman and scholar, died 1645
'By understanding many things I have accomplished nothing.'

•

I'm really good at bungee jumping...

Georg Wilhelm Hegel, German
philosopher, died 1831
– remaining philosophical to the last
**'Only one man ever understood me.
And even he didn't understand me.'**

•

Edvard Grieg, Norwegian composer,
died 1907
'Well, if it must be so.'

•

*Oh! Someone seems to have pulled out
the pin in this hand grenade...*

George Orwell, journalist and writer,
died 1949
– final entry in his notebook
**'At fifty, everyone has the face that
he deserves.'**

●

Courtlandt Palmer, founder of the
Nineteenth Century Club, died 1874
**'I want you to say that you have seen
a free-thinker die without fear of the
future, and without changing his
opinion.'**

●

*These are the safe kind
of mushrooms...*

Charles V, King of France, died 1380
**'I find that kings are happy but in this;
that they have the power of
doing good.'**

•

Bishop Pierre Pigneau de Behaine,
French missionary, died 1799
**'I willingly leave this world where I
have been thought happy in that I
have had public admiration, been
respected by the great, esteemed by
kings. I can't say that I regret these
honours – it's just that they add up to
vanity and trouble.'**

•

Nobody could get here that quickly...

Robert Drew, executed by lethal
injection 1994
'Remember, the death penalty
is murder.'

•

Henning von Tresckow, one of the
Stauffenberg plotters against Hitler. He
chose to commit suicide rather than be
executed, and killed himself with a
hand grenade in 1944
'The worth of a man is certain only if
he is prepared to sacrifice his life for
his convictions.'

•

*Listen, I know how to handle
a chainsaw...*

Mark Twain, American writer,
died 1910
'Death, the only immortal, who treats
us all alike, whose peace and whose
refuge are for all. The soiled and the
pure, the rich and the poor, the loved
and the unloved.'

•

Hans Frank, Nazi war criminal,
hanged 1946
'A thousand years will pass and the
guilt of Germany will not be erased.'

•

I bought this gun in the sales...

William H. Vanderbilt, American millionaire, died 1885 – puts it into perspective

'I have had no real gratification or enjoyment of any sort more than my neighbour down the block who is worth only half a million.'

•

Robert Alton Harris, executed in the gas chamber 1992 – his last words were taken from the film, *Bill and Ted's Excellent Adventure*

'You can be a king or a street sweeper, but everyone dances with the Grim Reaper.'

•

You are on my side, aren't you?

Benjamin Franklin, American
politician, diplomat, inventor,
scientist and writer, died 1790
'A dying man can do nothing easy.'

•

John Baptiste Dubois,
French diplomat, died 1742
**'Death is a law and not a
punishment. Three things ought to
console us for giving up life – the
friends we lost, the few persons
worthy of being loved whom we
leave behind us, finally the memory
of our stupidities and the assurance
that they are now going to stop.'**

•

I'm an expert at this...

Aleister Crowley, black magician and mystic, died 1947 – his autobiographical *Confessions* concludes with the following

'What may befall, I know not, and I have almost ceased to care. It is enough that I should press towards the mark of my high calling, secure in the magical virtue of my oath: "I shall endure unto the End."'

●

Sir Walter Ralegh, Elizabethan courtier, poet and explorer, beheaded 1618

'So the heart be right, it is no matter which way the head lieth.'

●

I wonder where its mother is?

Goodbye Cruel World
Unhappy Or Unwilling Adieus

Anonymous, of Louis B. Mayer,
Hollywood mogul, died 1957
**'The only reason so many people
attended his funeral was that they
wanted to make sure he was dead.'**

•

David Garrick, English actor and
dramatist, died 1779
'Oh, dear...'

•

They wouldn't dare...

Anonymous, unsuccessful actor, suicide
**'I tried so hard to make a comeback.
Exit, Act III.'**

•

Manolete, bullfighter, killed in
the ring 1947
**'I can't feel anything in my right leg.
I can't feel anything in my left leg.
Doctor, are my eyes open? I can't see!'**

•

Come on, I'm a very good driver...

Lionel Barrymore, son of American actor Maurice Barrymore who died in 1905 – as the straps lowering his father's coffin became twisted and the coffin had to be raised again to adjust them
'How like Father – a curtain call.'

•

Lytton Strachey, biographer and critic, died 1932
'If this is dying, I don't think much of it.'

•

Can we not drop our weapons and talk about this?

Margaret, daughter of King James I
of Scotland, died 1445
**'Death! Don't talk to me about
it any more.'**

•

Charlie Starkweather, mass murderer,
electrocuted 1959 – asked if he would
donate his eyes to medicine
**'Hell no! No one ever did anything for
me. Why in hell should I do anything
for anyone else?'**

•

*I'm just going to have a
look in here...*

Lope Felix de Vega Carpio, Spanish
playwright and poet, died 1635
**'All right, I'll say it.
Dante makes me sick!'**

•

George IV, King of England, died 1830
– to his page, Sir Walter Waller
**'Wally, what is this? It is death, my boy.
They have deceived me.'**

•

I've seen them do this on TV...

Jimmy Glass, executed by
electric chair 1987
'I'd rather be fishing.'

•

Jugurtha, King of Numidia,
died in a freezing underground
cell 104 BC
**'Oh Hercules!
How cold your bath is!'**

•

*You don't have the
guts to kill me...*

Lionel Herrera, executed by lethal injection 1993
'I am innocent, innocent, innocent. Make no mistake about this. I owe society nothing. I am an innocent man and something very wrong is taking place tonight.'

●

Fritz Sauckel, Nazi war criminal, hanged 1946
'I pay my respects to American officers and American soldiers, but not to American justice.'

●

Have you got a match?

Dr Alexander Blackwell, physician, printer and adventurer, beheaded 1747 – upon being corrected by the executioner for having put his head on the wrong side of the block

'I'm sorry for the mistake, but this is the first time I've been beheaded.'

•

Sir James Radcliffe, third Earl of Derwentwater, Jacobite rebel, beheaded 1716 – to his executioner

'I am but a poor man. There's ten guineas for you. If I had more I would give it to you. I desire you to do your office so as to put me to the least misery you can.'

•

It won't take me a moment...

W. Somerset Maugham, English writer
and playwright, died 1965
**'Dying is a very dull, dreary affair. And
my advice to you is to have nothing
whatever to do with it.'**

●

Melvin Fuller, American jurist, died 1910
'I am very ill.'

●

*Hey, I know that guy.
Wasn't he on* Crimewatch *last week?*

Last Rites
Deathbed Religion

Plotinus, Neoplatonic philosopher,
died AD 270
**'I am making my last effort to return
that which is divine in me to that
which is divine in the universe.'**

•

Simon de Montfort, Earl of Leicester,
English soldier and politician, killed at
the Battle of Evesham 1265
**'Commend your souls to God, for our
bodies are the foe's.'**

•

Are you sure it's not loaded?

Lucilio Vanini, Italian philosopher,
burned as a heretic 1619
**'There is neither God nor devil: for if
there were a God, I would pray Him to
send a thunderbolt on the Council, as
all that is unjust and iniquitous; and if
there were a devil I would pray him to
engulf them in the subterranean
regions; but since there is neither one
nor the other, there is nothing for
me to do.'**

•

Wilson Mizner, Hollywood wit, died
1933 – to his priest
**'Why should I talk to you?
I've just been talking to your boss.'**

•

Wow, you are really UGLY!

Brendan Behan, Irish playwright, died 1964 – to a nun who was taking his pulse just before he died
**'Bless you, Sister.
May all your sons be bishops!'**

•

Monsignor Ronald Knox, British religious writer, died 1957 – declining, when asked if he would like to hear a reading from his version of the Bible
**'Awfully jolly of you to
suggest it though.'**

•

*I love playing Russian roulette!
I've never lost yet!*

Rufus W. Griswold, Edgar Allan Poe's
literary executor, died 1857
**'Sir, I may not have been always a
Christian, but I am very sure that I
have been a gentleman.'**

•

Henry the Lion, Duke of Saxony
and Bavaria, died 1195
'God be merciful to me, a sinner.'

•

*OK, go ahead and
make my day...*

W. C. Fields, American actor and wit,
died 1946
– when observed flicking through the
Bible on his deathbed
'I'm looking for a loophole.'

•

Karla Faye Tucker Brown, executed by
lethal injection 1998
**'I am going to be face to face with
Jesus now...I love you all very much.
I will see you all when you get there...
I will wait for you.'**

•

I think it'll take my weight...

Vespasian, Roman emperor,
died AD 79
**'Woe is me, I think I am
becoming a god.'**

•

Baruch Spinoza, Dutch philosopher,
died 1677
**'God have mercy upon me
and be gracious to me
– a miserable sinner.'**

•

*These pills are pretty small.
I think I should take a few extra
just to be sure...*

Captain Frederick Marryat, naval officer,
inventor and author,
died 1848 – in the nick of time
'After years of casual, and, latterly, months
of intense thought, I feel convinced that
Christianity is true, and the only religion
that can be practised on this earth; that
the basis of Christianity is love; and that
God is love. To attempt to establish any
other creed will only, in the end, be folly.
But Christianity must be implanted in the
breast of youth; there must be a bias
towards it given at an early age. It is now
half past nine o'clock. World, adieu!'

•

Ludwig van Beethoven,
German composer, died 1827
'I shall hear in Heaven.'

•

Let's get him!

Pietro Perugino, Italian painter, died 1523 – refusing to send for a priest on his deathbed
'I am curious to see what happens in the next world to one who dies unshriven.'

•

John Eldon Smith, executed by electric chair 1983
'Well, the Lord is going to get another one.'

•

They'll never think of looking here...

Voltaire, French philosopher and writer, died 1778 – refusing, on his deathbed, to forswear the devil
'This is no time to make new enemies.'

●

Coventry Patmore, British poet, died 1896 – propagating a tough love, speaking to his wife
'I love you dear, but the Lord is my life and my light.'

●

That doesn't usually happen...

James Thurber, American humorist,
died 1961 (attributed)
'God bless...God damn!'

•

Saint Lawrence, Catholic martyr, died
AD 258 – on being burnt alive by the
Romans above a gridiron
**'Turn me. I am being roasted
on one side.'**

•

I don't think they've rumbled us...

Time For Reflection

Daniel Defoe, British novelist,
died 1731
'I do not know which is more difficult
in a Christian life – to live well or to
die well.'

•

Edith Cavell, British nurse, shot by the
Germans as a spy 1915
'I realize that patriotism is not
enough. I must have no hatred or
bitterness toward anyone.'

•

I hope this isn't a one-way street...

Anonymous German spy, shot by the
British 1914 – his last letter home

'My Dear Ones, I have trusted in God and
He has decided. My hour has come, and I
must start on the journey through the
Dark Valley like so many of my comrades
in this terrible war of nations. May my life
be offered as a humble offering on the
altar of the Fatherland. A hero's death on
the battlefield is certainly finer, but such
is not to be my lot and I die here in the
enemy's country silent and unknown, but
the consciousness that I die in the service
of the Fatherland makes death easy. The
Supreme Court Martial in London has
sentenced me to die for military
conspiracy. Tomorrow I shall be shot in the
Tower. I have had just judges and I shall
die as an officer, not as a spy. Farewell,
God bless you, "Hans".'

•

We've got the all-clear...

Philip III, King of Spain, died 1621
'Oh would to God I had never reigned.
Oh that those years in my kingdom I had
lived a solitary life in the wilderness. Oh
that I had lived alone with God. How
much more secure should I have died.
With how much more confidence should
I have gone to the throne of God; what
doth all my glory profit but that I have
so much torment in my death.'

●

Friedrich Froebel, German educator,
died 1852 – asking to be taken out
into his garden
'My friend, I have peeked at lovely
Nature all my life. Permit me to pass my
last hours with this enchanting mistress.'

●

*You know there's no such thing as
vampires...*

Barbara Graham, executed in the gas chamber 1955
'Good people are always so sure they're right.'

•

Marco Polo, Venetian merchant and explorer, died 1324
'I have not told half of what I saw.'

•

I won't fall off...

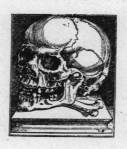

William Maxwell Aitken, first Baron
Beaverbrook, British press magnate,
died 1964 – his last
public statement
**'This is my final word. It is time for me
to become an apprentice once more.
I have not settled in which direction.
But somewhere, sometime, soon.'**

●

Franz Kafka, Czech writer, died 1924
– he asked for all his papers and
letters to be burnt
**'There will be no proof that I
ever was a writer.'**

●

*Thanks, but I'm not sure a plaster is
really going to help...*

David Zeisberger, American missionary,
died 1808
**'I have reviewed my whole life and
found that there is much to be
forgiven.'**

•

John Spenkelink, executed by electric
chair 1979
**'Capital punishment: them without
the capital get the punishment.'**

•

Don't worry, I've done this before...

Stoical Swansongs
Facing Death With Dignity

W. Graham Robertson, British author, died
1948 – final instructions
**'I should like the ashes to be buried or
otherwise disposed of at the crematorium,
with no tombstone nor inscription to
mark the place of burial. No funeral, no
mourning, no flowers. By request. If these
arrangements are carried out one may
perhaps manage to die without making a
public nuisance of oneself.'**

•

Cato the Elder, Roman statesman, writer
and orator, committed suicide 149 BC
'Shut the door.'

•

Do you think this lift is over-crowded?

Charles Lamb, English essayist, writer and poet, died 1834
'My bedfellows are cramp and cough – we three all in one bed.'

●

Edgar Degas, French painter and sculptor, died 1917
– instructing his friend and fellow painter Jean-Louis Forain about the arrangements for his funeral
**'But if there has to be a funeral oration, get up and say,
"He greatly loved painting. So do I."
Then go home.'**

●

That's odd...

Erskine Childers, Irish writer and
patriot, executed by firing squad 1922
**'Come closer, boys.
It'll be easier that way.'**

•

Benjamin Hill, US senator,
died 1882
'Almost home.'

•

*You wouldn't hit a man with
glasses, would you?
Er, would you?*

Charles II, King of England, Scotland and Ireland, died 1685 – referring to his mistress, Nell Gwynn
'Let not poor Nelly starve.'

•

Lieutenant Aloysius Schmitt, US Navy chaplain, killed at Pearl Harbor 1941 – he insisted on being last through the porthole to safety when his ship was bombed by the Japanese, and became stuck
'Go ahead boys, I'm all right.'

•

It must be dead by now, surely?

Theodore Roosevelt, American
President, died 1919
'Please put out the light.'

•

John Graham of Claverhouse, first
Viscount Dundee, Scottish soldier, killed
at the Battle of Killiecrankie, 1689 –
asked how the battle went he was told,
'Well for King James, bad for you'
**'If it goes well for him it matters
the less for me.'**

•

He's no match for me!

Harry Houdini, American escapologist, died 1926

'I am tired of fighting. I guess this thing is going to get me.'

•

Stephen Crane, American writer, died 1900

'When you come to the hedge that we must all go over, it isn't so bad. You feel sleepy, you don't care. Just a little dreamy anxiety, which world you're in, that's all.'

•

This tastes a bit odd...

Radclyffe Hall, British author,
died 1943
'What a life; but such as it is,
I offer it to God.'

•

Gouverneur Morris, American
politician, died 1816
'Sixty-four years ago it pleased the
Almighty to call me into existence here
on this spot, in this very room, and
now shall I complain that he is pleased
to call me hence?'

•

Er, maybe I shouldn't have done that...

Francis Buckland, naturalist and
Inspector of Salmon Fisheries,
died 1880
**'I am going on a long journey.
I shall see many strange animals on
the way. God is so good, so good to
the little fishes, I do not believe He
would let their Inspector suffer
shipwreck at last.'**

•

Vincent Van Gogh, artist, suicide 1890
**'Now I want to go home.
Don't weep. What I have done was
best for all of us. No use.
I shall never get rid of this
depression.'**

•

Ha! I don't think they'll try that again!

Thorstein Veblen, American economist, died 1929 – a farewell note

'It is also my wish, in case of death, to be cremated, if it can be conveniently done, as expeditiously and inexpensively as may be, without ritual or ceremony of any kind; that my ashes be thrown loose into the sea, or some other sizeable stream running to the sea; that no tombstone, inscription or monument of any name or nature, be set up in my memory or name in any place or at any time; that no obituary, memorial, portrait, or biography of me, nor any letter written to or by me be printed or published, or in any way reproduced, copied or circulated.'

•

Ned Kelly, Australian outlaw, executed by hanging 1880
'Such is life.'

•

Don't worry, whoever did this will be long gone by now...

Adam Smith, Scottish philosopher and economist, died 1605
'I believe we must adjourn the meeting to some other place.'

•

E. W. Scripps, American journalist, died 1926
'Too many cigars this evening, I guess.'

•

No – I thought you *were bringing the antidote?*

August Strindberg, Swedish dramatist,
died 1912
'Everything is atoned for.'

•

Charles-Maurice de Talleyrand-
Périgord, Prince of Benevento,
died 1838
'Do not keep me in suspense.'

•

Cover me...

John Tyler, US President, died 1862
'I am going. Perhaps it is for the best.'

•

Stanislaus I, King of Poland,
died of burns when his cloak caught
fire in 1766
**'You gave it to warm me, but it has
kept me too hot.'**

•

I never get lost...

Tamerlane, Turkic conqueror,
died 1405
**'Never yet has death been frightened
away by screaming.'**

•

General Sir Redvers Buller, British
soldier, died 1908
**'I think it's about time to go
to bed now.'**

•

Ha! I've got you now!

Marya Bashkirtseva, Russian diarist and painter, died 1884 – as she watched a candle go out beside her bed
'We shall go out together.'

●

Lucius Septimius Severus, Roman emperor, died AD 211
'Little urn, you will soon hold all that will remain of him whom the world could not contain.'

●

I'll jump down the hole to see how deep it is...

Steven Judy, executed by
electric chair 1981
**'I don't hold any grudges.
This is my doing. Sorry it happened.'**

•

Clarence Lackey, executed by lethal
injection 1997
'I love you, Mom.'

•

*I can't believe no one has ever
tried this before!*

Mario Benjamin Murphy, executed by lethal injection 1997
'Today is a good day to die. I forgive all of you. I hope God does too.'

•

Marie-Antoinette, queen consort of Louis XVI of France, guillotined in 1793 – to the executioner, after she stepped on his foot
'Monsieur, I beg your pardon.'

•

No, it's fine. I've not had that much to drink...

Henri IV, King of France,
assassinated 1610
'It is nothing.'

•

Samson, biblical hero, killed *c.* 1155 BC
'Let me die with the Philistines.'

•

Look, Mum! No hands...

Epitaphs

Asked to compose their own epitaphs...

•

He was lucky, and he knew it.
Cary Grant, film star, died 1986

•

Did you hear about my operation?
Warner Baxter, film star, died 1951

•

Excuse my dust.
Dorothy Parker, writer and wit, died 1967

•

Don't be so superstitious...

**Here's something I want to
get off my chest.**
William Haines, film star, died 1973

•

Do not disturb.
Constance Bennett, film star, died 1965

•

This is too deep for me.
Hedy Lamarr, film star, died 2000

•

*Aha! You can't outwit me – I recognize
your pistol as a cleverly disguised
cigarette lighter...*

Good friend, for Jesus's sake forbear
To dig the dust enclosed here!
Blessed be the man that spares
these stones,
And curst be he that moves my bones.
William Shakespeare,
dramatist, died 1616

•

A gentleman farmer goes back
to the soil.
Lewis Stone, film star, died 1953

•

Big deal. I'm used to dust!
Erma Bombeck, American writer,
died 1996

•

He should have run out of ammo by now...

Well, I've played everything but a harp.
Lionel Barrymore, actor, died 1954

•

**Psst! The guy next to me
isn't really dead...**
Anonymous

•

That's All Folks!
On the gravestone of Mel Blanc, famed
for his vocal roles as Bugs Bunny and
Sylvester the Cat, among others,
died 1989

•

I can get my whole head in here!

Tombstone
Humour

HERE LIES JOHNNY YEAST PARDON ME FOR NOT RISING

Ruidoso, New Mexico, USA

•

Don't worry, I think the Vikings are generally a very peace-loving people...

SIR JOHN STRANGE HERE LIES AN HONEST LAWYER, AND THAT IS STRANGE

England

•

Lightning never strikes the same place twice...

HERE LIES LESTER MOORE FOUR SLUGS FROM A .44 NO LES NO MORE

Boot Hill cemetery, Arizona, USA

•

*I don't think he'll mind if
I pull his beard...*

HERE LIES
EZEKIAL AIKLE
AGE 102
THE GOOD
DIE YOUNG

East Dalhousie, Nova Scotia, Canada

•

Have you got any grenades left?
Yes? Throw one across then...

ANN MANN – HERE LIES ANN MANN, WHO LIVED AN OLD MAID BUT DIED AN OLD MANN

London, England

•

It's only a couple of million pounds. Why's he so upset?

ANNA WALLACE – THE CHILDREN OF ISRAEL WANTED BREAD AND THE LORD SENT THEM MANNA, OLD CLERK WALLACE WANTED A WIFE, AND THE DEVIL SENT HIM ANNA

Ribbesford, England

•

Yes! We've made it!

HERE LAYS BUTCH, WE PLANTED HIM RAW. HE WAS QUICK ON THE TRIGGER, BUT SLOW ON THE DRAW

Silver City, Nevada, USA

•

They can't see me! I'm invisible!

READER IF CASH THOU ART IN WANT OF ANY DIG 4 FEET DEEP AND THOU WILT FIND A PENNY

Epitaph of John Penny,
Wimborne, England

•

Don't try to scare me. You don't even know how to use that thing...

HERE LIES AN ATHEIST ALL DRESSED UP AND NO PLACE TO GO

Thurmont, Maryland, USA

•

Watch this...

SACRED TO THE MEMORY OF MY HUSBAND JOHN BARNES WHO DIED JANUARY 3, 1803. HIS COMELY YOUNG WIDOW, AGED 23, HAS MANY QUALIFICATIONS OF A GOOD WIFE, AND YEARNS TO BE COMFORTED

Vermont, USA, written by the deceased's widow

●

I'll just take a shortcut down this dark alley...

I WAS SOMEBODY. WHO, IS NO BUSINESS OF YOURS

Anonymous, Vermont, USA

•

The odds of that happening are a million to one...

SHE ALWAYS SAID HER FEET WERE KILLING HER, BUT NOBODY BELIEVED HER

Richmond, Virginia, USA

•

Help, this oil well is on fire!
Someone get some water!

ON THE 22ND OF JUNE - JONATHAN FIDDLE - WENT OUT OF TUNE

Hartscombe, England

•

I don't care. They can do what they like...

HERE LIES THE BODY OF OUR ANNA DONE TO DEATH BY A BANANA IT WASN'T THE FRUIT THAT LAID HER LOW BUT THE SKIN OF THE THING THAT MADE HER GO

Enosburg Falls, Vermont, USA

•

*No problem, I'll just explain to this escaped
murderer that he's made a mistake...*

GONE AWAY OWIN' MORE THAN HE COULD PAY

Epitaph for Owen Moore,
London, England

•

It's probably just a rash...

IN MEMORY OF
BEZA WOOD
DEPARTED THIS LIFE
NOV. 2, 1837
AGED 45 YRS.
HERE LIES ONE WOOD
ENCLOSED IN WOOD
ONE WOOD
WITHIN ANOTHER.
THE OUTER WOOD
IS VERY GOOD:
WE CANNOT PRAISE
THE OTHER

Winslow, Maine, USA

•

Oh, lifejackets are for wimps...

UNDER THE SOD
AND UNDER
THE TREES
LIES THE BODY OF
JONATHAN PEASE.
HE IS NOT HERE,
THERE'S ONLY
THE POD:
PEASE SHELLED OUT
AND WENT TO GOD

Nantucket, Massachusetts, USA

•

I never miss...

HERE LIES MY WIFE: HERE LET HER LIE! NOW SHE'S AT REST, AND SO AM I

John Dryden, English dramatist (1631-1700), on his wife

●

We're home and dry...

HERE LIES ALL THAT REMAINS OF CHARLOTTE BORN A VIRGIN, DIED A HARLOT. FOR SIXTEEN YEARS SHE KEPT HER VIRGINITY A MARVELLOUS THING FOR THIS VICINITY

Welland, Ontario, Canada

•

I want to kill something...

All Michael O'Mara titles are available by post from:

Bookpost, PO Box 29, Douglas, Isle of Man IM99 1BQ

Credit cards accepted.
Please telephone: 01624 677237
Fax: 01624 670923
Email: bookshop@enterprise.net
Internet http://www.bookpost.co.uk

Free postage and packing in the UK.
Overseas customers allow £1 per book (paperbacks)
and £4.00 per book (hardbacks)

Other Michael O'Mara Humour titles:

All Men Are Bastards – ISBN 1-85479-387-X pb £3.99
The Book of Urban Legends – ISBN 1-85479-932-0 pb £3.99
The Complete Book of Farting – ISBN 1-85479-440-X pb £4.99
Complete Crap – ISBN 1-85479-313-6 pb £3.99
Shite's Unoriginal Miscellany – ISBN 1-84317-064-7 hb £9.99
The Ultimate Book of Farting – ISBN 1-85479-596-1 hb £5.99
The Ultimate Insult – ISBN 1-85479-288-1 pb £5.99
Wicked Cockney Rhyming Slang – ISBN 1-85479-386-1 pb £3.99
Wicked Geordie English – ISBN 1-85479-342-X pb £3.99
Wicked Scouse English – ISBN 1-84317-006-X pb £3.99
The Wicked Wit of Jane Austen – ISBN 1-85479-652-6 hb £9.99
The Wicked Wit of Winston Churchill – ISBN 1-85479-529-5 hb £9.99
The Wicked Wit of Charles Dickens – ISBN 1-85479-047-1 hb £9.99
The Wicked Wit of John F. Kennedy – ISBN 1-84317-057-4 hb £9.99
The Wicked Wit of Oscar Wilde – ISBN 1-85479-542-2 hb £9.99
The World's Stupidest Criminals – ISBN 1-85479-879-0 pb £3.99
The World's Stupidest Graffiti – ISBN 1-85479-876-6 pb £3.99
The World's Stupidest Inventions – ISBN 1-84317-036-1 pb £5.99
The World's Stupidest Laws – ISBN 1-85479-549-X pb £3.99
The World's Stupidest Men – ISBN 1-85479-508-2 pb £3.99
The World's Stupidest Signs – ISBN 1-85479-555-4 pb £3.99
More of the World's Stupidest Signs – ISBN 1-84317-032-9 pb £4.99
The World's Stupidest Chat-Up Lines – ISBN 1-84317-019-1 pb £4.99